Treasu Under the Sea

Isabel Thomas

Schofield & Sims

Have you ever seen reefs on television? They are full of living treasures!

Even the beautiful coral is alive. Let's dive in for a closer look...

Reefs are made by tiny animals called corals.
Most corals prefer tropical waters.

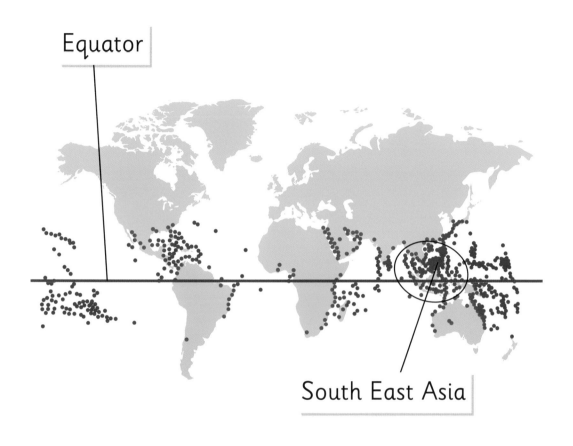

Equator

South East Asia

There are some wonderful reefs in South East
Asia, which is near the Equator.

Divers explore reefs for pleasure. They have torches to give them better vision underwater.

Turning on the light reveals an amazing rainbow display!

Reefs are full of food and hiding places. Unsurprisingly, many different animals live here.

Dazzling fish of all sizes dart about. Sea stars crawl slowly across the coral.

Every animal has its own way to find food.
This is a cleaner shrimp.

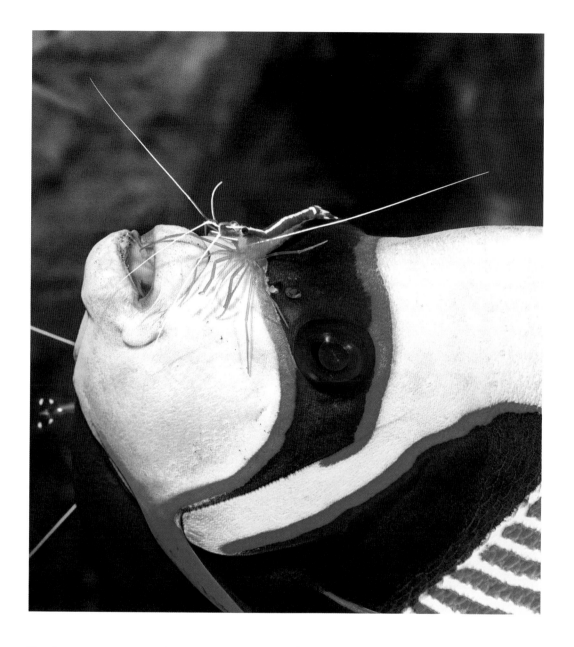

It hops onto larger animals and nibbles at their dead skin and germs!

Sharks and turtles visit reefs to find prey to hunt. Some animals swim away quickly.

Other animals have spines for defence.
Giant clams simply snap their shells shut!

Fact
Giant clams can live for
up to one hundred years!

Corals are tiny animals themselves.
They construct hard homes to hide in.

They stick their tentacles out to catch plankton that floats past.

plate coral

brain coral

staghorn coral

When a coral dies, its hard home is left behind.

Fact
Reefs grow more slowly than your fingernails!

New corals construct their homes on top.
Over time, the reef grows.

Reefs are one of the planet's most important treasures. They protect thousands of different animals.

They also protect shores from erosion. But corals
need protection too.

Every year, scientists measure how healthy reefs are. They have found out that coral reefs are under threat from:

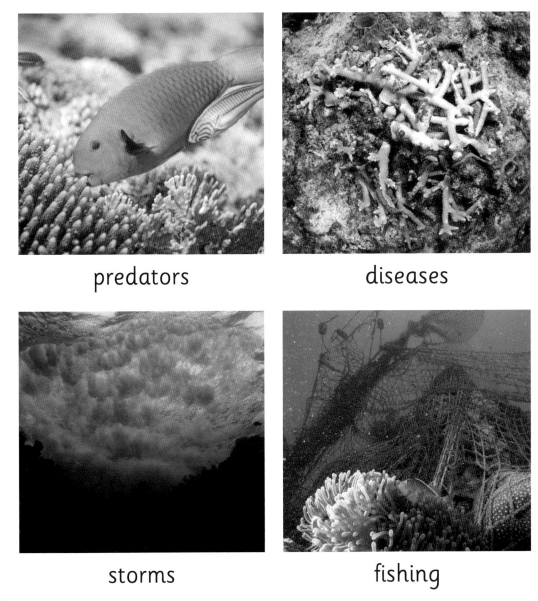

predators

diseases

storms

fishing

collisions with boats

people who collect coral

exposure to chemicals

seas heating up

Global heating is making seas heat up too. When corals heat up too much, they become unwell.

They may turn totally white. Reefs can recover, but this takes years.

We can all help to protect reefs by living more carefully.